NO CONFESSION,

Prairie Schooner Book Prize in Poetry   EDITOR Kwame Dawes

NO MASS

JENNIFER PERRINE

University of Nebraska Press   Lincoln and London

© 2015 by the Board of Regents of the University of Nebraska

Acknowledgments for the use of previously
published material appear on pages vii–viii, which
constitute an extension of the copyright page.

Library of Congress Cataloging-in-Publication Data
Perrine, Jennifer.
[Poems. Selections]
No confession, no mass / Jennifer Perrine.
pages; cm. — (Prairie schooner book prize in poetry)
ISBN 978-0-8032-7723-6 (pbk.: alk. paper)
ISBN 978-0-8032-8497-5 (epub)
ISBN 978-0-8032-8498-2 (mobi)
ISBN 978-0-8032-8499-9 (pdf)
I. Title.
PS3616.E7924A6 2015
811'.6—dc23
2015018770

Set in Quadraat by M. Scheer.
Designed by N. Putens.

Contents

III

IV

Acknowledgments

I extend grateful acknowledgment to the many editors who have continued to support my work. In particular, I thank the staff of the following journals, in which these poems first appeared, some in earlier forms:

The Account: "Envy | Kindness" and "Humility | Pride"

Adrienne: "Diligence | Sloth"; "The Divorcée's Fable"; "Greed | Charity";
    "I Would Rather Die a Thousand Deaths"; "Ode to the Motorcycle";
    "Seconds"; "Self-Portrait as Francis Bacon"; and "Song of the Bystander"

AGNI: "A Theory of Violence [—for Ciudad Juárez]"

Bellevue Literary Review: "After My Mother's Death, I Feel Nothing"

Bellingham Review: "Call Me" and "Love Song with Condemned Building"

Connotation Press: "Lust | Chastity"; "Mobility"; and
    "The Mystic Speaks of Attachment"

Crazyhorse: "Invocation: The Blessed Girl, after Her Visions and Vows" and
    "Patience | Wrath"

Driftless Review: "Pastoral for Our Uncharted Territories"

dsm Magazine: "The Mother, the Girl, the Mirror That Speaks"

Extract(s): "To Chant Back the Summer" and "Wow and Flutter"

Georgetown Review: "Elegy for My Morbid Curiosity" and
    "Happiness: from *hap* (fortune, luck)"

iO: "Dead Letter"

The Journal: "'Tis of Thee"

Meridian: "Piblokto"

Natural Bridge: "Coronal" and "For the Lone Man at the Violence Prevention Center"

New Ohio Review: "Embarrassment: from *baraço* (halter)" and
    "A Theory of Violence [In the museum of sex . . .]"

North American Review: "Letter to Half a Lifetime Ago"

Paterson Literary Review: "Wild Child (Slight Return)"

The Pinch: "Invocation: [Saint] Euphrosyne" and "Invocation: [Saint] Pharaïldis"

Redivider: "Fishwife"

Revolution House: "Temperance | Gluttony" and "Yoke"

River Styx: "Confidence Game"

Third Coast: "Lust"

"A Theory of Violence [— *after New Delhi, after Steubenville*]" first appeared as a Poem of the Week on the website of Split This Rock. "Invocation: [Saint] Genevieve" first appeared as the winner of the Tor House Prize for Poetry on the website of the Robinson Jeffers Tor House Foundation. I owe sincere thanks to both organizations, especially to Sarah Browning and to Elliot Ruchowitz-Roberts, for creating such welcoming spaces.

Deep gratitude to U.S. Poets in Mexico and to the Kimmel Harding Nelson Center for the Arts for residencies during which I wrote the earliest poems in this book; to the Vermont Studio Center for a fellowship that provided me the generative and contemplative space in which this manuscript began to take shape; and to Drake University for a sabbatical leave that allowed me time to focus and finish this work. I also offer my heartfelt appreciation to the editors at *Prairie Schooner* and University of Nebraska Press for believing in this book and giving it a home in the world.

Thank you to my many colleagues and students who inspire me and remind me to keep seeking the hope-kissed places. Long overdue thanks to all the teachers who showed such kindness toward and patience with the person I was half a lifetime ago, especially Jeannie Zeck, Saundra Morris, Cynthia Hogue, and Harold Schweizer. My ongoing gratefulness to the friends whose conversation, insight, and wisdom help me think through the tough questions, both in life and on the page, particularly Tyler Mills and Susanna Childress. And love, again and always, to Justin Huck, proof of my good fortune, my unbelievable luck.

NO CONFESSION, NO MASS

I

Invocation: [Saint] Genevieve

In worship, the people remember you

                    as a protector, invoke you to guard

against natural disasters: drought, flood,

                    sweat of fever. To recall your power

to heal they must bring to mind your abuse:

                    how your mother struck you—her heavy palm

sharp against your face—and as punishment

                    lost her sight until, months later, you fetched

water from a well, washed her eyes, lifted

                    the veil from her world. How did your mother

look in that moment, engaged in her own

                    mystic vision, returned from her journey

in the dark? What did her gaze light on first:

                    the fragile fabric you daubed at her lids,

the small coin you wore tethered at your neck,

                    your long fingers reaching toward the girl

you would become, who ate only barley

                    bread and beans, slowly paring your body

into that relic, enshrined, borne aloft

                    through the streets of Paris, sucking poison

from believers, drawing out the ergot,

                    the gangrene from their hands and feet? What prayer

was poised on her lips in that instant, spell

                    to keep you safe, to stop the villagers

from begging at your bones? Did she wish you

                    desire, a spouse, arms spangled with trinkets,

enough excess to extinguish the fire

                    a bishop lit in your seven-year-old

self? Is she the one who sits forever

                    beside you in the icons, in disguise

as the devil, her breath a stinging rush

                    of wind at your cheek, her bellows huffing,

fervent, trying to blow your candle out?

The Mother, the Girl, the Mirror That Speaks

What choice does the woman make, inspecting
her face at dawn, the mirror flanked by bulbs
that transport her from clear *day* to dusty
pink *evening*? The girl suspects the gentle
rouge of twilight, where the dial remains

after her mother has left with layers
of creamy pancake armoring her skin.
What flaw, what damage does she try to hide,
bandage, seal tight with powder? What power
does the glamour hold? The girl doesn't know,

but all those hours, days until her mother
comes home, she gazes into the silver
square like Narcissus snared by his image
in the pool, his hair twining its tendrils
toward the surface as he stares, rooted

to the place while Echo calls, calls, waits
for vanity to unbind its slick shine,
to release her beloved to the sharp
rock that lurks in the shallows, the soft kiss
of sand buried too deep to see, aching

for touch. Even the water says, *Enter
me*, beckons to the girl, *Closer. I can
carry you from this place. I'll show you where
your mother's gone. Watch her eyes, your lips sink
into the dusk. Slip into me, and trust.*

To Chant Back the Summer

of us, three lazy queens

        enshrined on plastic lounge

                chairs, our long hair dreaded

with chlorine. Never bored,

        we planted our sun-flecked

                selves like hostas in shade

by the poolside, or grew

        less domestic, tube-topped

                honeysuckle, two-toned

when nude, flowers opened

        by the evening, fragrant

                pollen waft in the dusk.

At dark, we'd shut the screen

        doors tight against neighbor

                boys, the hollow echo

of basketballs smacking

        pavement. They'd assign us

                bawdy names—we'd replace

them, ink one another

        with markers, arms tattooed,

                each others' signatures

set like jewels in crowns

        of arrow-riddled hearts.

                At midnight, we'd return

outside, tumble like rocks

        tossed in the creek, our backs

                to the boards of the deck,

our chests pressed rib to rib

        to rib, or else belly

                down in the just-mown grass.

We'd fill and be full, breath

        spiced like cider, that tart

               of apple and sharp scent

of clove that would whisper,

        liquid, the faintest hint

             of our oncoming fall.

Humility | Pride

In the dark before dawn, in the drawn-out
heart of August—month made to impress
my skin with its lack of restraint, no shame

in its salt-sweet sweat, its scrub of chiggers—
I lay in the cleared field, arms lifted, hands
pressed against the sky to catch the shower

of stars that were not stars but lofty rocks
spun from space, incandescent with friction,
that swept me with streaks of light, glitter

strewn on my body's parade, holiday
celebrating this first moment I knew
the worth of witness, the use of my shy,

watchful self, who loved being low, treasured
how I, too, was a small speck sent whirling
in surrender, a mote of brilliant dust.

For the Lone Man at the Violence Prevention Center

Agonies are one of my changes of garments
—Walt Whitman

You were in her shoes, high-heeled boots
much too big for eight-year-old feet,
so you shuffled your way across
to the mirror where you draped fringed
gauze scarves from your head, pretend hair
cascading over your shoulder.
Twelve years later, you try in vain

to explain this day to strangers:
It's not that I wanted to be
a girl. No, I'm not gay. You say
you didn't need to know the silk
of her dress, the ritual of blush,
lipstick, and perfume to make sense
of the pleasure of adornment,

of costume. You only wanted
to unearth why, when your mother
walked with you to school on her way
to work, she'd turn her face, avert
her eyes from men in cars who'd sing
their endearments — *baby, sweet thing* —
and screech away or sometimes slow

their pace to a crawl, watch, silent.
This, you tell us, is why you marched
out into an afternoon garbed
in her entire ensemble, clomped   .
careful steps around the one block
where you were allowed to venture
alone. When the first stone hit you,

you fell, the scrape of the sidewalk
tearing your knees, hose. By the time
you stumbled home, boots and scarves tossed
in bushes, ribs kicked and crushed, mouth
full of mud, you knew the culprits:
kids who played hide and seek with you
in backyards, girls and boys who skipped

rope, battled each other with sticks
poised as swords. After, your mother
wept for days, made you swear *never*
again, chased off the ones who threw
dirt clods as you sat on the stoop,
moved you both to an apartment
in the next town. You rode a bus

to your new school, and she took one
to work. You never saw the men
whoop and holler at her again,
but you still wear her flinch inside,
you tell us now. In the quiet
after, we wear it, too, recall
our own walks in our mothers' shoes.

Embarrassment: from *baraço* (halter)

All he found when he came looking for us was the home my mother wanted to leave behind: newspapers stacked knee-deep in the hallways, every corner redolent of cat piss, linoleum caked with dried mud and dust, tangles of hair matted to the tub, dried scabs of meals coating plates and bowls piled high in the sink, on counters. Everywhere the stink, the rot and mold, the great heaps of unwashed clothes, all the filth my mother never let anyone see. No friends allowed inside. Even her dates didn't get in the door. She spent her nights at their dubious dens, leaving me alone to toss hamburger wrappers and soda cups on the living room floor, our one trashcan so full I couldn't empty it. My father, finding all this mess, assumed the worst, took photos, jotted notes, thinking the house had been ransacked, that we'd been robbed, killed or kidnapped, though police assured him there were no signs of struggle. How she'd let the house go, he couldn't imagine. Before the divorce, I heard her shout: *I'm no one's maid.* Years later, when my father asks how we lived in such squalor, I tell him I never noticed at the time, though once I did: My best friend, Heather, and I were playing outside when a sudden shower drove us to huddle under the eaves. Soaked, I took pity, opened the door, disobeying my mother's one rule. Inside, Heather didn't ask questions about the mildew, the crumpled paper bags she had to brush aside to sit. She refused the towel I handed her to undo the work of the rain. I saw it then: tatty, gray, stained. Heather left, and later, when my mother found the couch still wet, I told the truth. Her face flushed; I tried to bolt. She reined me in with one hand, unfastened her belt. *If they see this, they'll take you from me,* she screamed through the volley of blows. My back grew a rope of welts. *They'll call me unfit. Is that what you want?* I tell my father none of this, judge it best not to show him the last bits of how his ex fell apart once they were unhitched. I don't say how I, too, was the mess, tether she yearned to slip, so she could careen unimpeded through life, how I held tight as she zoomed away, raced toward a place where she'd be no one's mother, no one's wife.

Envy | Kindness

My hand pressed to her stretched skin,
her full belly turns a key

without a room, climbs ivy
through my empty insides, vines

that twine this trellis of need.
I lower my eyes, green seed

germinating in my veins,
blood pumping with little knives,

the thousand cuts of this Ides
made of each mother I've seen,

from paintings of gravid Eve
to my own mom, with seven

kids, to this dear friend who sends
me sonograms. I deny

to her the screech of this vise
winding tight at her joy, sink

my keen howls in an inky
deep. For her I unspool skeins,

knit blankets, stay by her side
at doctor's visits, devise

a surprise shower. Still I
can't stifle this yen. I kiss

it, cradle it, hush its din,
cries that echo in the den

where nothing grows, nothing dies.

After My Mother's Death, I Feel Nothing

except heartburn, or more precisely,

                                   in the doctor's words,

you've grown a hole

                    where the acid leaks through

and floods up into your mouth,

and now I know

                 the truth's come out:

this is how love's always felt:

                           ignition switch in my chest

    and whatever revs to life

emits neither subtle hum nor purr

                  nor growl.

There's no word for it—no yawp, no howl—

                           only a taste, a texture:

bilious twitch pushed wrong-way through

                    this faulty valve.

    I've wanted so long to love the way

                      others proclaim—

through praise and grief,

               through speaking aloud the beloved's name—

but mother, I have only this—

                 cells that once divided

                          inside you

now run amok, consumptive,

this pulse at my throat

turned sharp blue flame.

If I knew where to find you,

I'd bury it beside you,

I'd pull out the fuses, the wiring,

this whole damned

machine,

let its fuel

wash over you,

let it unmark

your grave.

Invocation: [Saint] Euphrosyne

After *ascetic* but before *austere*

comes *attire*, as in: the way to escape

when, at ten, you're already affianced

to a stranger known only for his wealth

is to be reborn, to bury beauty,

cloister it in a monk's cowl, to carry

out the coveted body like washing

and beat it against a rock, cold water

tearing at the jewelry of your face.

Whatever shimmer of sex might have slept

safe in you, inhabited the welcome

country of youth, you offered, oblation

at the altar of change, burnt all your names —

daughter, desire, despair — until you ceased

to be woman, became instead servant,

disciple who drove even the abbot

to distraction, the elders unable

to overcome their longing, confessing

how you'd slip into their dreams, surprise them

even when pious, awake, until peace

arrived for you only in solitude,

cell where you were no temptation at all,

where you spread your limbs the length of your rough

bed and prayed, where only God could witness

your grace, only joy would answer your call.

A Theory of Violence

—after New Delhi, after Steubenville

Under the surface of this winter lake,
I can still hear him say *you're on thin ice*
now, my heel grabbed, dragged into the opaque
murk of moments—woman raped on a bus;

girl plunged into oblivion, taken
on a tour of coaches' homes, local bars,
backseats of cars, the sour godforsaken
expression on each classmate's face; the dark,

the common route home, faint footfalls behind.
How many times have I bloodied my fist
against this frozen expanse to remind
myself there is another side, hope-kissed,

full of breath? I howl. The water begs, *drown*,
its hand pressing tight, muffling every sound.

The Divorcée's Fable

Call it what you will—park, garden,
domesticity—I'd been bred

to be docile, to allow hands
to touch, to feed. No one would say

I met neglect or cruelty,
only it was clear who had made

the display, the menagerie,
who had built enclosures and moats

around me. So when a stranger
unlocked my cage, I did not bite,

I did not flee. No squeal, no squeak
to mark the day I was removed,

set down feral in the forest
for my slow untaming. My zoo

habits free, I crept in the wild,
my shoddy bones learning to roam

the roadless expanse, to survive
solitude, space, wonder at last.

But even here the threat is clear—
I have grown my pelt thick with fear

of being hunted, sold as drug
or food, or worse yet, of meeting

the ones who would name me *stray, lost*,
make of me the beloved pet.

Song of the Bystander

You quaffed the whole bottle and then, for good
measure, shattered its glass against the bar,
littered the floor with slivers. Someone should
have balked, but the room spun around you, star

bright center, laughing too loud as you slammed
your palm down, burying one glinting shard.
You didn't scream, only cursed the goddamned
beads of blood, cheap rosary, then fell hard,

blacked out on the warm wood. Your ponytail
swung as some man lifted you, unaware,
over his shoulder. Your hand dripped a trail
as he hauled you into the raw night air.

The door shut on you, him, the spilling snow.
No one followed. We watched. We let you go.

Piblokto

In winter, you arrived, your voice as strange
as those of ice and stone. You spoke of me
        as sad girl, pool of snowmelt in which you
glimpsed your own frost-rimed face. Later, you tried
        to part my legs and found a snapping cur

that rent your rutted flesh and, blizzard-blind,
        bolted naked into the three-day drifts.
When I returned, icicles strung like fur
        about my throat, you deemed me mad: Arctic
hysteric, womb frozen, floating, a berg

        carried out to sea. Still, in my stupors
and seizures, you followed me, curious
        about my dog disease, my wild brooding.
Explorer, you've found a phantom in me—
        come stand in my circle, shake to my scream,

watch how I become the one with the drum,
        pinioned to prevent flight just long enough
to let the spirits dance through me—they speak
        your senseless words I've overheard, echo
uncontrolled. Come, ghost in our midst, leering

        at our wheeling fits. Come, we invite you
to our feast—tonight we dine on organ
        meats. For you, the fish, the mammal livers:
we need no augury to divine this
        distance between sickness and resistance.

A Theory of Violence

—*for Ciudad Juárez*

I march to a slow, careful beat:
the pace of my heart, each harsh leap.
Let the sun-warmed bricks burn my feet.

Here, where death and silence repeat,
the day goes slack—time crawls, I creep,
I march to a slow, careful beat

over stone, sand, broken concrete,
past mouths pressed shut, secrets they keep.
Let the sun-warmed bricks burn my feet.

My skin flares red. The monstrous heat
lifts fine blisters that burst and weep.
I march to a slow, careful beat.

The path will never be complete,
for we have sown. Now we will reap.
Let the sun-warmed bricks burn my feet.

At night, I sweat through my thin sheet,
dream each step. Even while I sleep,
I march to a slow, careful beat,
let the sun-warmed bricks burn my feet.

'Tis of Thee

Sweet land of laboring, I am your sheep,
bleating in your concrete pastures,
offering myself up for shearing, let me
be fleeced. Let me be husbanded, herded.

Of thee I sang-froid, I calm at your terror
scale. When your flags fly up
and your ordure comes down, I anchorite,
I cloister, by my own hand penned.

Land where my fathers did work
themselves to death, did walk on
and strike rockets at the moon, did chop
cherry trees, did not tell lies.

Land of the pills, grams, pried open
mouths, I swallow you down: much
madness is assent. I spoon full of sugar.
I medicinal merry-go-round.

From every mountain's hide I neon
my home, revere your glow, applaud
your bootstrap plots, your melting pot,
how it oils my tongue, let free, dumb.

Greed | Charity

In purgatory, penitents are bound,
immobile, laid with faces pressed
down, gazes fixed upon the ground
as they contemplate every excess.
We thrill to imagine their holy distress,
take pleasure in the sufferings
Dante conjured, horrors meant to impress
us, sate our love for earthly things.

We enter the fire a crude compound,
sizzle until we incandesce,
until we're nothing but a mound
of gold, stripped of the dross of worldliness.
Origen's metaphor doesn't hold unless
we ignore our end: coin clutched in the purse strings
of God. Still, we ask the divine to assess
us, sate our love for earthly things.

Whatever peace we may have found
through our acquiring, our largesse—
how our generosity astounds—
harbors the low rumble of pain we repress,
afterimage of the dispossessed
we try to shake, but our senses cling
to the hoardings, petty thefts that possess
us, sate our love for earthly things.

We don't trick, manipulate—simply say *yes*
when offered our due share as conquerors, kings,
and with grace, tip our crowns as we beg, *bless*
us, sate our love for earthly things.

Mobility

Begin with the dreams
    where you're once again
a teen, alone, a strange
    city to navigate
without a map: the network
    of trains, buildings that turn blind
eyes as you pass, crisscross of streets
    without signs. Fumble inside: halls
that lack doors, elevator that lifts
    to an unmarked floor, opens to rooms
of raucous men, women's red laughter. Now
    you've entered, there's no way back out—only
two kids in the corner—greasy-haired, tattooed—
    who beckon you close, so you crouch low, listen
as they whisper, *We're squatters here, too.* The warm wet
    air creeps over your skin as the dresses and suits
exhale mirth and gin, and against the thin reedy sound
    of it all, the firm whack of your boot against the wall,
pounding a steady, heady thump that breaks through the chatter,
    interrupts the revelry, and as the two kids join, feet
and fists cracking plaster, forces a silence, a hole, a breach.
    The faster you beat, the more sunlight pours in, until you've hacked
a wide, terrible grin, a maw into which you lean, an exit
    into wind that tears at all the people climbing the facade, picks
and ropes, the slow hoist, the vast haul yet to go, and you no longer know
    whether you still want out, or to pull everyone in, or to tear down
the whole shining structure, level its concrete and glass, raze its wonder, leave
    not even a glimmer of that once distant place for you to remember.

Patience | Wrath

I have broken the bridge over which I must pass
but kept the splinters housed safe in my skin —
they send shivers of pain that I cannot forgive.

I coax them free: needles to sew a cloak, a shroud.
I mimic the mim seamstress, pressing pins
in my mouth. I wait long as it takes, prim-lipped pose

meant as dupe, as disguise, so you do not notice
this pomegranate part, this striker held
in place by my coy arts, so you take it as play

when you tug at my safety, ignite this reserve,
lob it aloft, then witness as it burns
churches, rattles bones, robs you of breath and mother,

of God and home. I revel this fiery glory —
let the blaze grow uncontrolled. You thought *fool*,
not *foe*, so by your own hand your ruin is sown.

A Theory of Violence

In the museum of sex, the video loops
its cycle of common bonobo behavior:
penis fencing, genital rubbing, whole groups

engaged in frenzied pairs, their grinds and shrieks
playing for the edification of each patron
passing through the room. We all summon

our best poker faces. One woman speaks
softly, reads from the sign that describes
all the various partner combinations,

the multitude of positions, how relations
lower aggression, increase bonding within tribes.
We linger over this way of making peace,

wonder to each other if we would cease
our litany of guns, bombs, missile strikes
if we spent more time in wild embrace.

The exhibit doesn't mention our other cousins,
chimpanzees, who form border patrols, chase
strangers in their midst, leave mangled bodies as lessons.
That's the story we already know

and want to forget through the release
of these erotic halls, where we seek the thrill, the bliss
of these animals who hold us captive
while we lament what traits we've found adaptive.

Invocation: The Blessed Girl, after Her Visions and Vows

Your hand to your heart, you knew how to play
       the part, to read the faces of your marks,
their belief in your continuous fast,
       how you ate nothing but the Eucharist,

but I saw the flour pinched in your fingers,
       ragged rind cupped in your palm, your eyes fixed
on the sick, the poor, while your mind, dark dove,
       winged toward God, or toward the impure,

the sweet secreted behind a red sheet,
       your body pricked by a cartload of thorns,
by his admiring gaze upon your hair—
       magnificent, he'd said, twining himself

there—your friar called you his divine heir,
       then died, left you wounds you could not undo
except by tearing your tresses, wrenching
       them by the roots, beauty shorn for ugly

truth, letting legend replace your labor:
       you cried out just once, not from worldly pain
but to name the agony of angels
       tying a cord around your waist, twisting,

binding you so tightly they could pull you
       to your feet, let you walk away silent,
your penance complete, little spirit left
       naked, trembling—of which you'd never speak.

Self-Portrait as Francis Bacon

begins with a photo of me, age seventeen, at a party
that called for fancy dress. In drag, I went, stripped my cuffs
and collars and donned a flapper's beads and heels, lipstick, cigarette
smoldering in its opera-length holder—I could not have been bolder, loose
woman exposing myself for the camera, lens like a mirror in which I watched
gender whip to and fro—silk tie, silk slip—I hid them both in the cramped closet:
that cupboard was the making of me.

                                            begins with the scream, locked in the cabinet
where I studied colored plates of oral disease, gazed at one still from a silent
film—close-up of a wounded nurse, broken spectacles askew, the stain
of unheard terror—I opened that mouth again and again, on faces
of innocents and nocents, all the names I could not make for
my sinister self, unprimed, always on the wrong side:
that man who paints those dreadful pictures.

                            begins
with my lover's death, or my lover himself, who emerged
like a Fury, born from blood and genitals flung into the sea—
no goddess on a shell for me—I prefer my deities chthonic, vengeful,
waists entwined with snakes, or human—black-robed mourners, damsels
in short skirts and boots, the gracious ones, the kindly ones who stalk my triptych:
daemons, disaster, and loss.

Letter to Half a Lifetime Ago

Dear girl waiting outside, alone,
    just tossed out of your parents' house:
        I offer this age's adage—
            it gets better. Sometimes it does.
        Other people's mothers will take
    you in, admit the sin's to leave
a kid on the streets, but they'll turn,

too, when they find your fingers twined
    in their daughters' hair. You'll seek bars
        where you don't get carded, linger
            under the beneficent reign
        of queens who bring you to diners
    in the wee hours, make sure you eat.
You'll play pool with butches who teach

you to flick your lighter open,
    chivalrous, although you don't smoke,
        how to shave your head when barbers
            won't, what to do when men eye you
        in a parking lot, hurl insults,
    then rocks. You'll learn the exact size
of bruise left by a fist, the shape

of the girl who lifts you, carries
    you to her car, her home, lets you
        sleep while she cooks you eggs and toast.
            She'll lend you book after book, whole
        pages underlined, where you glimpse
    worlds of two women together,
fictions where they do what they please

with their lives, and still they survive.

   When she declares you *just a friend*,

      you'll write your gloom and grief, won't cry.

         You'll drink until your mind's scrubbed clean,

      then test sobriety at clubs

   where you press sweat to sweat to bass

and drums. You'll wear studded leather,

white tanks, black boots: signals that say

   both *fuck off* and *come here*. You'll fall,

      gobsmacked, and they'll fall, too: broken

         beauties, motorcycle chicks, punk

      princesses, gynoanarchists.

   Each time, you'll buzz with kisses

you wish wouldn't stop, embraces

in the midst of busy sidewalks,

   bustle around you forgotten.

      Each will leave you waiting, cast off,

         alone again, but now knowing

      this isn't the end, that you'll see

   your way through with one long, steady

stride, and the next one, and the next.

Love Song with Condemned Building

In your absence, I lick your photo. Film
slicks liquid, and I call you water, drop
that swims the nape of my neck. I call you
rainstorm gathering along the cape, good
hope distant as a half moon at midday
or close as the sun striking this window
I call skin, begging to come in, to prize
open what wants to be locked. This house full
of hollows — pockets in a patchwork dress,
clay pots, bottles quaffed in one swift swallow —
I call it fugitive, place you hid, space
where you left only this image, now wet,
where you called nothing but my name, your tongue
in this room, surfacing, urgent as breath.

Lust

Evolution undone, you spit venom
    that makes me go donkey. I seethe and froth,

        snapping at my handler. I am the dog
        that needs watching (the dog bites your leg), buzz

        at your throat (the mosquito bites your neck).
    I lurch through scrub in search of berry juice,

    sluice of sweet red. The woodcutter litters
        the road with my bones, the old crone buries

        my teeth. You trip along with your basket,
    chance upon my skin. You feed me morels,

  I thirst for something warm in which to swim—
    a blood brigade, pool full of gin. I grow,

flourish, all of me edible—shoots, leaves,
  tubers, roots, flowers, fruit—little black pods

        that erupt, inking daydresses, nightgowns,
    with this artless hunger in which we drown.

Call Me

slut, slag, slattern, sleaze—I won't bat one lash,
just slip my hand beneath your shirt, slalom
down the slope of your chest, sled on a sheet
of sleet, careening, sleek, just out of sight.
Your slang's no slight—it's a slogan: I'll slurp
you down, cherry slush, slobber neon juice,
sleuth your fruit, or I can be your sloe-eyed
slice of lime, Singapore sling, silk skirt slit
to the thigh. Slug me, swig me in one go,
slosh my sludge in your red innards—I'll slur
your words, slam you through slumbering city
streets, sail you on this hurricane sloop, fore
and aft, slander your slot, just the right slant,
your thighs a sledge, your head a slash, until
you go slack. I'll slink out but still remain:
through slats in your sleep, my peepshow will play.

Lust | Chastity

Desire works its sliver, splinter,
      snag that undoes my lace,
a hurried unfurling, a gaze
      shot through a prism, your face

multiplied, magnified, your voice
      rumbling in the echo
chamber of my brain, how it swells
      like a river, this slow

current hastened by rain, dragging
      me swift around the bend,
your whisper a murder, water
      that drowns. No way to mend

what's rent, cover this coveting,
      this swoopstake, cropneck want,
this ghost that stalks all my shadows,
      crouches in every haunt

where I try to hide, to escape
      your moan, a growing hymn
that muffles the murmur of vows
      barely remembered, dim

distant beacon flashing from shore.
      It's no promise that keeps
me from the plunge, the risk of flood,
      lungs full, diving your deeps—

only I know the liquid thrum
     I've imagined—the lick
of salt where your shoulder meets throat—
     would be undone. Our quick

fingers would swallow all sound save
     the roar as we combust,
burn through every stitch, our conjured
     thrill now ebbing, now dust.

Yoke

Pressed to my tongue like a pill, a Eucharist, you wake in me
this spark and spur. Dear, dread catalyst, you wake in me.

You frame a house of ash and ember, offer only hollow
smoke until I beg for the blaze, insist you wake in me.

After sex, sweat collects at your sternum, rainwater
pooled, placid after the tempest you wake in me.

Your hair loops, whorls in the sink, the shower. I fill a room
with its straw, set spinning the alchemist you wake in me.

In the gold purse of morning, I find origami stars
that mimic each practiced turn, each twist you wake in me.

You tear each flower from its stem as if this could undo
the bloom, forestall fruit, withhold the harvest you wake in me.

I see you now, glinting, coin tossed in a fountain.
Single wish that's gone unnoticed, you wake in me.

You wrap the blindfold tight, lead me to a room of steel
implements where I swear, honest, you wake in me.

Tonight you wear all your teeth, don your finest claws,
release a beast to roam the forest you wake in me.

You appear as archangel. As serpent, too. Either way,
I cast you out, invoke the exorcist you wake in me.

Drunken god, you pursue me. Salvation means I turn to stone.
Contrite, you weep wine, gloss of amethyst you wake in me.

You crook my arm into this hook, this pivot and punch
I did not know I owned, the swinging fist you wake in me.

Fair phantom, you wander from room to room in the dark,
master of obstacles. Somnambulist, you wake in me.

Wild Child (Slight Return)

There's nothing for it like coming back
seventeen years later
to the place you lived at seventeen—
the in-between when you left home
for unknown roads, miles of city
streets after the subway closed.

I say *you*, but of course I mean *I*,
that time meant to launch a life
instead spent starving, the bones of my hips
lifting from my jeans, reaching
from beneath the coat in which I smuggled
my body with its new, hard art—

art of walking face-first
into wind, into snow,
art of fucking only men
who had wives, girlfriends,
art of passing out on trains,
coming to with my shirt undone,

a stranger over me, art of learning
to tell women I loved them, art
of hitching a ride hours in the dark
to see the ocean, art of paring
the self down to one bright,
unrepentant, unadorned

thread, art of vomiting loudly
and alone, art of waking
early, art of longing, art
of wanting to be elsewhere,
art of knowing there is no
there there, art of dancing

until exhaustion, until failure,
until you, that is *I*—
not confessing but unearthing—
unbolted, flew open
and had no fear, until I called,
and the word was not *help* but *here*.

I Would Rather Die a Thousand Deaths

The sum of splendor stings:
    I drink joy, its fleet blades tucking furrows
that flourish in my muscle, incisions
    that loose glimmers —
        fine, feathery folds that thrash my back.

Some sights are cudgels swinging easy, tinny jingling of keys in the dark —
        the incessant affair of capture and care.

Beauty beheads me — no petty beating — instead, the impending guillotine
    a divorcing: ritual of crown and blade,
        elegant touch
    of rust in the sleek slash.
A single blink: my heart rent from its rest.

I am the stars that storm out,
    seduced into the hairpin turn,
        the boldness of the eternal thrill.
    This wonder hurts,
        sings, purrs,
            smuggles me aboard,

then howls, strikes me down
    until I beg, *please, more*. In its force, I am blown from what holds me fast.
    I surrender to this riot. May it mark me. May it last.

Ode to the Motorcycle

Not even parked in a proper garage,
you rest in a plywood shed, wheels half sunk

through the dirt floor. At fifteen, I wanted
more than the bitch seat as I rode two up

with a man twice my age, knowing only
to lean into turns — never how to steer

or shift or brake easy. I learned to wear
the gear — creased leather chaps, silver buckles —

not how to grease bearings and tighten bolts.
I longed for you even then: black and chrome,

the jolt of wet leaves, gusts, debris, oil slicks
that would teach me to close my grip, absorb

the shock, wait out the slide. Fifteen more years
would pass before I gathered the courage

to find you, ride you alone on summer
nights, gravel roads. By then I'd grown too old

to need four hundred pounds of steel to prove
my boldness, to prefer your rumbling roar

to the hushed gutturals of my own voice.
I'll miss the heat rising from your engine,

the visor dark enough to let me hide.
Still, I've made my choice: five years you've rusted,

crusted over with webs and pollen, soft
parts split open where the mice nest. Thank you

for reminding me how I let you die:
beast that would have helped me flee my troubles,

that would have rattled numb my fists, my thighs,
would have sent me round the bend, let me fly.

Dead Letter

Dear acclimation to adolescence,
to aerobics and aerosol, dear age
of consent, dear abandon, dear all-night
altercations, dear array of ashtrays,
arabica, aspartame, dear artless
auditions for antidepressants, dear
avarice, dear annus horribilis
(advent of anomia), dear abyss,
dear anyone, anytime, anywhere,
anywise, dear auld lang syne: au revoir,
aloha, adieu, adios, avaunt.

IV

Invocation: [Saint] Pharaïldis

What scholar gave you this improbable

                name, so awkward it sprains my tongue? Who found

the need to translate *Veerle*, so lilting,

                so easily a fountain from the mouths

of your Belgian kin—even your parents,

                who nearly did you in, gave you away

for gold; even your husband, who beat you,

                said he was owed his due, though you refused,

spent nights in church until the miracle

                of your widowhood. Veerle, let me build

a cult around whatever word you like,

                let us speak of your will but of wicked

justice, too: how even after your death,

                misers would touch your tomb and find their bread

turned to stone. Maybe you'd choose *Medusa*,

                your relics rattling, skeletal cackle

each time their teeth touched the loaves, or *Helen*,

                beauty beyond reason, for the moment

when you cradled a goose—plucked, cooked—gathered

                her bones, whispered them back into her skin,

then restored her breath, stroking your fingers

                through the new plumage, and returned her whole,

startled raw, launched her back into the world.

Pastoral for Our Uncharted Territories

When we came to this place, I whispered, *Here*
be dragons,
              but saw in the field only
dragonflies, ancient flitting creatures plucked
from some absinthe dream.
                        We walked out, barefoot,
and I could feel the green
                  beneath, my skin
stippled by those slender blades, and later,
my knees dyed, stained.
                   This is the home we make,
cherries left for birds to suck, small apples
we pocket or let drop and rot.
              Far off,
houses fill the whole horizon, windows
dark, but here I watch
                our sleek black dog glide
over the garden fence, the rabbits flushed
from their burrows, darting across the grass.

This is the spot where you taught me
                    birds' names—
starlings roosting in the hedges, common
grackle, whose title belies
              its feathers,
iridescent, its song a creaky hinge.

In winter I note their cupped nests,
                empty,

just below where the sun crests, crimson haze
spooled out behind; across the way,

                         vacant

baseball diamonds, the flagpole stripped, rattling
its rope in the wind.

               In that cold sometimes
I forget this grin, this you, tanned, sweat-slick,
tilling earth and clearing weeds.

                      I forget
to marvel at our cellar doors, rust-red
handles always raised, as if tugged by ghosts
seeking shelter;

             I welcome them, remind
myself we're never alone, remember
when we arrived you said,

                  nothing stays owned.

Fishwife

I imagined you would come as ocean,
iridescent bouquets of open shells—

how you'd drape me in curtains of kelp, sparks
of sand flaming on my skin—but I know

now how I swam to your shore, breath beating
in the creel of my lungs. My thighs still shed

scales, hyaline windows through which you peer,
on which you raise tongues of steam. In the dark,

you sneak fingers to those deep green slivers.
I move in the shelter of your dry land.

Temperance | Gluttony

At the dim sum parlor, while my mother
　　　devoured full plates of bao, steam exhaling
　　　　　as she broke open each fluffy white mound,
　　　I held back, allowed only a mouthful
of soft dough, bright sweet meat. I knew to keep

room for the slick chew of wide rice noodles
　　　and one delicate har gow: burst of shrimp,
　　　　　translucent skin pinched into a seashell.
　　　I regarded each passing cart with calm
control, not risking the big bowl of thick

congee, nor the pile of crimson chicken
　　　feet my mother called phoenix claws. Flavors
　　　　　sold at the local strip mall—pot stickers,
　　　egg rolls—went untouched while I sought secrets
lifted from bamboo baskets: lotus leaf

triangle, its subtle earth scent infused
　　　into the sticky heap that hid sausage
　　　　　and slivers of mushroom. I plucked single
　　　morsels, unfamiliar chopsticks fumbling,
sipped chrysanthemum tea, petals blooming

with warmth, watched the stamps collect on our card.
　　　Last to my tongue: an inch of taro cake,
　　　　　fried dollop of red bean paste. How that strange
　　　array mixed in my belly as at last
we spilled into late morning on Mott Street,

its wallop of baffling talk, of sun-splashed
      awnings as we walked through wafts of garbage,
          fish markets, the mystery of city
      scents. Years later, I will recall for you,
new love, this whole excursion, fine balance

I found to temper temptation. I'll urge
      restraint—just a taste, the smallest nibble,
          one tiny bite. I'll teach you all I know
      of the strap of savor, harness of feast,
how bridle and rein kindle appetite.

The Mystic Speaks of Attachment

The mystic sits at the front of the hall,
cross-legged, intones, *Attachment prevents*
us from real love. As if one body, all
our heads bob up and down, nod our assent

to his wise words. We each want to open
wide to another, no need for control
or possession or desire's keen talon
we've honed to rip, to rend, leave nothing whole.

After, in the bathroom, the mystic's wife
leans against the sink, studying her arms
in the mirror. On each, an angry welt

flares. When she spots me staring at the scars,
she holds them out: faint tattoos that once spelt
names of old lovers, scraped off with a knife.

Confidence Game

Dear quacksalver, dear honey-tongued, I beg
        a draft of the tonic atop your case,

I trade my bones for your balm, for your best
        flimflam cure—do not ask me what it's for.

It's for this palimpsest, this parchment vest,
        how I try to cover, to erase this

original text, bound in my body,
        the past a subtle poison, a tender

spot in the breast. Dear slick-suit, dear shined-shoes,
        send word of the way to scrape the traces

of earlier forms, pitch me your finest
        Lazarus pill that I might be reborn

or—not so tied to the divine—at least
        reused, free from my malady, what ails

me, complaint of constraint, to be saddled
        with my old selves, bit and rein. Dear huckster,

dear hawker, dearest predator, I pray
        peddle me your wares. I will believe them

no sham. Dear trickster, dear lover, I'll quaff
    any green glass you hand me, trust you can

mix the elixir that will ensure me
    this transformation, this alakazam.

Wow and Flutter

Once, I shook to another's mix, spinning
in stereo, honeyed hymns so hungry

they sent me rolling and tumbling, crying
as the boom box rode shotgun those long road

trips of youth, during which I discovered
the wow and flutter, unpredictable

speed that at best left me singing a step
ahead of the music, my voice too real,

too bold to slow for poor fidelity,
at worst chewed, unspooled me, until I tore

away the tangled mess, slung its slickness
into the shoulder, ditched its serpentine

shine and its magnetic song, and I slipped
in a new cassette, pressed play, and drove on.

Diligence | Sloth

In the meditation chapel, we sit
motionless as gargoyles, eyes soft, lidded,
grotesquerie of blank faces hidden.

The final words of the Buddha—*strive
on*—serve as whips and spurs, jolts that drive
us to practice detachment from life.

We wait for nothing. We persist
with precision, skilled machinists
lathing the mind, watching it waste,

how the inner workings slow,
become slender. All we know
is breath. Let even that go.

Elegy for My Morbid Curiosity

Drop it, he says, as if I'm a dog
who's unearthed some half-decayed carcass,
swinging from my crude jaws its mottled

skin. It's true, I've disinterred again
the buried memory of his ex.
When we met, the grave still shallow, fresh—

only three months since she'd left—he spoke
of wanting to let go, to sever
the few remains of their oath—co-signed

loans, her name beside his on one last
set of checks. Now, three years out, we've shone
searchlights into our murky depths, dredged

and displayed for each other salvaged
bits of treasure from previous wrecks.
Still, he won't mention her. I worry

my key in that door, seeking a peek
into his life before she poured deep
the draught of doubt that lodged in his throat.

Though he's no Bluebeard and I'm no wife,
whatever I might find in that room
is secret, taboo. The bloody past

tempts only me. Even so beguiled
by the scent of rot, once more I tongue
the silence, then—for good—let it drop.

Happiness: from *hap* (fortune, luck)

—*for Huck*

All these years later, his favorite mug reads *Happiness is* IRAQ *in my rearview mirror*,
blue sky and clouds around the letters, a heaven in the windshield, the one way he
celebrates that he came back in one piece, at all. Though I wasn't there at the time,
didn't even know he existed, sometimes my breath still hitches with relief—how
easily we might never have met, a single mortar erasing the nights we've spent
folded into each other, simple evening bliss of crosswords and cooking together
gone. The unhappening of our mingled life clicks noisily, ratchet played in my skull,
hatchet wielded by the *what if*, cleaving me messy as wet wood. These are the
instruments of fear—rough music of canteen and rucksack, boots beaten against sand,
jangle of battle rattle. I blot them out, tear empty-handed at the master's house,
kick at the pillars, pummel fists into brick, into panes of glass, unhinge the doors,
let grass fill the space where men cocooned his body in camo and hoped for
metamorphosis. Thank god there was less magic in their wish than in his impish
name, that mischief marched with him day after uniform day. Some nights,
over a second or third beer, he boasts of the games he could make of their rules:
PT sessions when he'd mosey the two miles in desert heat, while everyone else
quickened their pace, tried to break thirteen minutes in full gear. *Why the hell would I
run? What's the worst they could have done—sent me home?* He laughs at himself, *bad soldier*,
shakes his head at all his buddies who sprinted ahead, his smile as he recalls it a small
triumph, suggesting some part of the rebellious boy they deployed remains
untouched. Still, when he says *happiness never lasts*, his words strap me into a ballistic
vest, tuck me under a combat helmet soaked thick with sweat, so that even now, as
we lie in bed, flesh pressed to flesh, his thumb brushing lazy circles on my knee, some
x'd out memory hovers between us, a mirage shimmering in the dark—the ghost of his
young face unburdened, curly hair not yet shorn short, the way he wore it before
zero hour, before the Operation, surgery that left him with no visible mark.

Coronal

You call me *darlin'*—not as I'd say
hon or *sugar* to sweeten my tips,

not flirting, but with a touch of flint
meant to burn away my given name,

hook plucked from a trend, a book. You know
to summon a truer term than *dear*

or *beloved*. Let me hear the husk:
blues you utter, palm cupping my breast,

and at my nape, the balm of your breath.
I savor the placement of your tongue

at the end, not velar, body pressed
to the soft palate, but coronal,

made with the blade tucked behind the teeth—
a harder sound saved for the private

space where our words take shapes less formal,
less round, where we balance on the sharp

brink, this point, this peak where you uncoil
a crown with your mouth, lay it on me.

Seconds

Bless this table, bought secondhand,
its wood the color of butter,
its sturdy surface plain and round,
a little worn, stripped of luster.

Bless its silence: so many fights
we brought to its ring. Bless its space,
barrier it made while we slogged
through the dreck of old wounds, new pain.

Bless how it never gave the close
fit of our bed, nor the comfort
of the couch, your head in my lap.
Bless how it broke open each word

we feared to speak, how when you left
for two weeks, I didn't eat, stared
at the empty seat, played your song,
crooned along: *And you make it hard.*

Bless how it heard our quiet vows
when you returned, how this table
waited for the day we would bet
on who'd be the first to dribble

on the just-washed cloth, when we could
joke about how you still chow down
with military speed. Bless late
nights, cards, beer, how it stuck around

while we conjured our recipes:
cioppino, slow-simmered curries,
stews, and Sunday morning pancakes
and eggs, when I pour you coffee

and you fix my tea. Bless these years
we've shared our simple joys, our blues,
how this table sings of offered
seconds: *What have you got to lose?*

In the Prairie Schooner Book Prize in Poetry series

Cortney Davis, *Leopold's Maneuvers*

Rynn Williams, *Adonis Garage*

Kathleen Flenniken, *Famous*

Paul Guest, *Notes for My Body Double*

Mari L'Esperance, *The Darkened Temple*

Kara Candito, *Taste of Cherry*

Shane Book, *Ceiling of Sticks*

James Crews, *The Book of What Stays*

Susan Blackwell Ramsey, *A Mind Like This*

Orlando Ricardo Menes, *Fetish: Poems*

R. A. Villanueva, *Reliquaria*

Jennifer Perrine, *No Confession, No Mass*

To order or obtain more information on
these or other University of Nebraska Press
titles, visit nebraskapress.unl.edu.